Coming of Age

Mandy Ross

Heinemann Library
Chicago, Illinois

© 2004 Heinemann Library
a division of Reed Elsevier Inc.
Chicago, Illinois

Customer Service 888-454-2279
Visit our website at www.heinemannlibrary.com

Designed by David Poole and Geoff Ward
Originated by Ambassador Litho Ltd
Printed in China by Wing King Tong

08 07 06 05 04
10 9 8 7 6 5 4 3 2 1

**Library of Congress Cataloging-in-Publication
Data**
Ross, Mandy.
   Coming of age / Mandy Ross.
      p. cm. -- (Rites of passage)
Summary: Explains the origin, historical or religious
significance, and practice of coming of age in different
cultures around the world.
Includes bibliographical references and index.
   ISBN 1-4034-3986-9 (lib. bdg.) -- ISBN 1-4034-2511-6
(pbk.)
   1. Initiation rites--Juvenile literature. 2. Adulthood--
Juvenile literature. [1. Initiation rites. 2. Coming of age. 3.
Rites and ceremonies.] I. Title. II. Series.
   GT2485.R67 2003
   392.1'4--dc21
                        2003001896

Acknowledgments
The author and publisher are grateful to the following
for permission to reproduce copyright material:
Cover photograph: Ralph A. Clevenger/Corbis.
p. 4 Images of Africa; p. 5 David Young Wolff/ Getty
Images; p. 6 Jonathan Blair/Corbis; p. 7 David Arnston/
AP; pp. 8, 9 Piers Cavendish/ Impact; p. 10 Chris
Lisle/Corbis; p. 11 Link Magnum Photos/Abbas; p. 12
Adrian Arbib; p. 13 Hutchison Picture Library; p. 14
North Wind Picture Archives; pp. 15, 19 Andes Press
Agency; p. 16 Penny Tweedie/Corbis; p. 17 Richard
I'Anson/Lonely Planet Images; p. 18 Yasha Mazur/
Israelimages.com; p. 20 Ann & Bury Peerless; p. 21
Christine Osbourne; p. 22 South American Pictures;
p. 23 Patrick Ward/Corbis; p. 24 Tadashi
Kajiyama/Impact; p. 25 Bill Wassman/Lonely Planet
Images; p. 26 Hulton-Deutsch Collection/Corbis; p. 27
Christine Osbourne/Circa; p. 28 Popperfoto/Reuters;
p. 29 Chuck Savage/Corbis.

Special thanks to both the Interfaith Education Center in
Bradford, England, and Georga Godwin for their help in
the preparation of this book.

Every effort has been made to contact copyright holders
of any material reproduced in this book. Any omissions
will be rectified in subsequent printings if notice is given
to the publisher.

Some words are shown in
bold, **like this.** You can find out
what they mean by looking in
the glossary.

Contents

What Are Rites of Passage?

As you get older, you go through important life changes. These changes include growing from childhood into adulthood, marrying, having children, and dying.

All around the world, people gather to mark these changes with friends and relatives. Often, they carry out **rituals,** such as saying prayers, performing activities, or celebrating with dancing or a party. These rituals or celebrations are called rites of passage.

Coming of age

This book explores some rites of passage that mark the time when a child becomes an adult, or coming of age.

These Maasai boys in Tanzania are wearing special clothing as part of their coming-of-age ceremony.

There are many different ways of celebrating coming of age. Some are religious **ceremonies,** welcoming a young person as a new adult member of a faith. Others are based on day-to-day life—for instance, starting to teach young people things they will need to know as adults, such as work skills or how to provide food.

At a coming-of-age ceremony, a child starts to leave behind the world of childhood and takes a step toward a new stage of life as a young adult. He or she is getting ready to join a new group—the adult world.

Coming of age is celebrated some time between the ages of 12 and 21. This girl is celebrating her eighteenth birthday. Many cultures believe that eighteen is the age when a child becomes an adult.

Rites of passage

In 1909, Arnold van Gennep wrote about rites of passage. He made up this term to mean events that mark important times in a person's life. He said there are three changes in every rite of passage:
- leaving one group,
- moving on to a new stage,
- and joining a new group.

Holy Communion and Confirmation

Holy Communion is a way **Christians** remember the Last Supper, the meal shared by Jesus and his disciples on the day before he died. Many **Roman Catholic** children celebrate their first Holy Communion at the age of seven. Special prayers are said, and each person is given a wafer or piece of bread and a sip of wine.

Girls and boys take their First Communion together. Girls often wear a white dress, while boys dress in a shirt and tie. In some ways, the **ceremony** is like a wedding. The children are promising themselves to Jesus, and promising to live as good Christians. The ceremony **symbolizes** that they are now full members of the Christian church.

These Roman Catholic boys and girls have just received their First Communion.

Confirmation

In the Roman Catholic, **Methodist,** and **Anglican** churches, young people may be confirmed. Confirmation usually happens between the ages of twelve and sixteen, when they are considered old enough to understand Christianity and choose to be a Christian. They are confirming their parents' and godparents' promises—made at their **christening** or **baptism**—to bring them up as Christians.

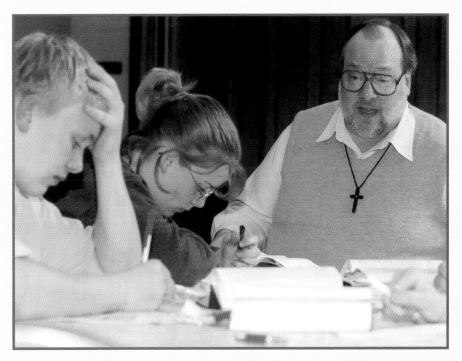

Teenagers prepare for their confirmation in the United States. At their confirmation they will promise to follow the teachings of Jesus Christ.

Melanie's story

Melanie, a Catholic, remembers her First Communion:

I went to classes to prepare for First Communion. We read stories from the Bible and learned about Jesus' life. On the day of my First Communion, I loved dressing up, having my hair done and wearing new shoes with silver buckles on! But I remember it was a serious and special day. I was given my own little prayer book so that I could say my prayers along with the adults.

Entering a Buddhist Monastery

In countries such as Vietnam, Thailand, and Burma, most of the people are **Buddhists.** In Buddhist countries, young boys may spend some months or years in Buddhist **monasteries** to learn more about Buddhism. In countries like Thailand, almost every boy does this. Girls can enter a Buddhist **nunnery** for some time, too, although fewer girls do so.

Boys can enter a monastery at any age. Most boys wait until they are about eight or ten years old. The boy's head is shaved to **symbolize** a fresh start. He wears simple orange robes, like the other **monks.** His daily life is just like that of a grown-up monk. He helps with jobs such as cooking or cleaning and has lessons in Buddhism and ordinary school subjects. After his time in the monastery, the boy returns to live with his family to work or continue with his education.

Young boys live as monks in a Buddhist monastery in Thailand.

These young boys in a procession are going to enter a monastery in Burma.

In Burma, there is a special **ceremony** for a boy entering a monastery. He leaves his home wearing his finest clothes, riding on horseback. It is a symbol of Buddha, a prince who went out from his palace to search for understanding. Then when the boy reaches the monastery, he takes off his fine clothes as a symbol that the Buddha left behind his life as a prince to teach about Buddhism. Instead, the boy will wear the simple robes of a monk.

Muslim Hatum Ceremony

Every day after school, many **Muslim** children go to classes at their mosque, the Muslim place of worship. They start some time between the ages of five and seven years old.

At the mosque they learn about Islam (the religion of Muslims) and the Qur'an (kor-AN), the Muslim **holy** book. Each day, they read a few verses of the Qur'an. After they have been going for two or three years, they may be ready for their *Hatum* **ceremony.** This ceremony marks the time when someone has read all of the Qur'an from beginning to end.

These children are at a class in the mosque. They are learning to read the Qur'an.

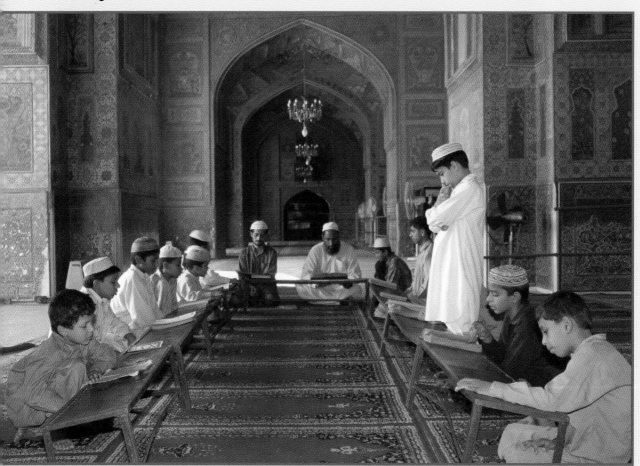

Fasting at Ramadan

Another sign of growing up comes during the Muslim month of Ramadan. During Ramadan, adult Muslims fast during the hours of daylight. In other words, they do not eat or drink anything from sunrise to sunset. From the age of seven, Muslim children start by fasting for just a few days each Ramadan. Gradually, they fast for more days each year, until by the age of twelve, they are expected to fast throughout the month, just like the adults.

This girl is learning the Qur'an by heart.

Farrah's story

Farrah Rehman is a Muslim girl from Birmingham, England. Here, she remembers her *Hatum* ceremony:

When I was ten years old, I was ready for my Hatum. I felt really nervous, even though I'd been practicing. My mom came with my sister and nieces and nephews. I read aloud the last ten surah, or verses, of the Qur'an. All my class listened as I read. I did make a few little mistakes, but my teacher sat with me, and she corrected me. When I finished, everyone said, 'Marsh'allah!'' which means 'Well done!' We brought sweets and rice for everyone in my class. I felt so happy that I'd finished reading the Qur'an.

African Initiation Ceremonies

In many ancient, traditional cultures, **initiation ceremonies** mark the time when a child enters the adult world. Often this change happens at the time of **puberty**—that is, when girls' and boys' bodies change as they become adults.

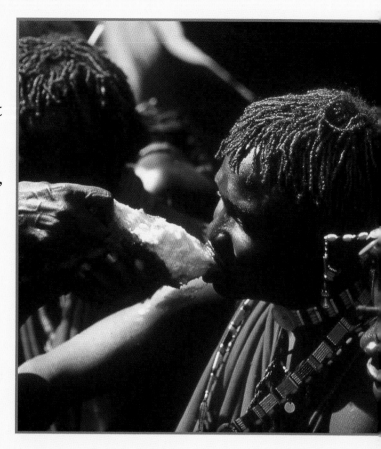

These boys are eating bull fat as part of their initiation ceremony in Kenya, in eastern Africa.

Haggai's story

Haggai remembers his initiation ceremony in Kenya when he was fourteen:

*Before the ceremony began, we built a hut in the forest far from our village. The women sang to encourage us to be strong and brave. Then, all of the men of the tribe gathered to watch our **circumcision**. It was very painful, but bearing the pain shows that you are a man.*
We lived in the hut for three months. Elders from our tribe taught us skills we would need as adults, such as hunting for food. Afterward, we were welcomed back into our tribe as men. I looked forward to my initiation, even though I knew it would be hard, because I was ready to become a man.

There are many different initiation ceremonies across Africa. Most of them emphasize that at puberty, boys and girls are starting to leave their childhood behind. They are becoming part of the adult community.

Girls' initiation rites

There are different initiation rites for girls. In parts of Zambia, in southern Africa, a ceremony called " dancing the chisungu" marks a girl's coming of age. The headman of the tribe blesses the girl by calling to the spirits of beloved **ancestors.** Then each day for several weeks, the girl performs **ritual** dances. These dances **symbolize** traditional ways of catching fish, making clay pots, and other skills that she will need as a grown woman.

This girl is dressed for her initiation ceremony in Sierra Leone, Africa.

13

Native American Sunrise Ceremony

After the Europeans arrived in North America in the seventeenth century, many Native American customs were no longer allowed. Today, however, Native American families in the United States are reviving some of the ancient **rituals.**

Many girls of the Apache (a-PATCH-ee) tribe, in the southwestern United States, have a four-day coming-of-age ritual. The ritual is called the sunrise **ceremony.** It is held in the summer after the girl's first **menses.**

The family chooses a godmother for the girl. The godmother will have a special relationship with the girl throughout her life. Before sunset, the godmother dresses the girl in special animal-skin robes decorated with feathers, beads, and shells. At this time, the girl is believed to have special healing powers.
Many Native American ceremonies and gatherings were banned by European settlers.

Changing Woman

The sunrise ceremony acts out the Native American **myth** of the first woman, known as Changing Woman. The myth tells how she survived the great flood and gave birth to two sons. When she grows old, Changing Woman walks east toward the sun until she meets her younger self, and then she becomes young again. Each girl dances the part of Changing Woman during her sunrise ceremony. In this way, according to the myth, Changing Woman becomes a part of every new **generation** of young women.

At her sunrise ceremony the girl must dance for up to six hours through each day and each night. It is a very long, hard test of the girl's strength. Her godmother dances with the girl to help her.

By the end of the ceremony, many girls feel proud of their strength and how long they danced. They feel ready to start taking on adult responsibilities.

*At her sunrise ceremony, this girl is covered in white pollen, which is considered **holy.***

Aboriginal Puberty Rituals

Many **aboriginal** peoples in Australia hold **rituals** at **puberty,** to prepare boys for manhood. The Walbiri people of central Australia hold a ritual for groups of up to fifteen boys.

The elders of the tribe decide exactly when the boys are ready, usually between the ages of eleven and thirteen. The boys go to live for a while in the bush, the wild and dry landscape of inner Australia. They are leaving their childhood world behind them, living apart from their parents and families.

The boys' bodies are painted with ochre, a natural red or yellow dye. The leader of the **clan** leads the boys in dances. The elders of the tribe tell the ancient stories of the Dreamtime, the aboriginal time of **myth.** These stories teach about practical tasks, such as hunting and using herbs for healing. The stories also teach about how society should be organized.

An aboriginal boy prepares for his initiation ceremony.

The most important part of the **initiation ceremony** is **circumcision.** It is a painful ritual, but it is important for the Walbiri people that the boys go through the pain. Shedding blood **symbolizes** the "death" of childhood, as the young men are "reborn" into the world of manhood.

The initiation ceremony happens for two reasons. It brings young boys into manhood, and it preserves the traditions and stories of aboriginal clans.

A girl grinding stone into powder. The powder will be used to make traditional aboriginal art.

Learning about aboriginal art

Aboriginal paintings, made out of natural materials, such as bark and vegetable dyes, also tell the stories of the Dreamtime. Many aboriginal artists are women. When their daughters are growing up, these artists teach them how to paint the traditional paintings of their clan or family, so that they can keep the traditions alive.

Jewish Bar and Bat Mitzvah

When a **Jewish** boy is thirteen, he can become bar mitzvah to mark the beginning of being an adult. In many synagogues (Jewish place of worship), Jewish girls become bat mitzvah when they are twelve or thirteen. In some **Orthodox** synagogues a number of girls share a bat chayil celebration instead.

Most Bar and Bat Mitzvah **ceremonies** take place in the synagogue. Usually, the ceremony forms part of the weekly service on Saturday morning. The young person is called to the front of the synagogue. Then he or she reads aloud from the Torah, the Jewish **holy** book. The Torah is written in Hebrew, the language of Judaism, on a scroll (roll of paper).

This Israeli boy is carrying the Torah before his bar mitzvah ceremony at the Western Wall, in Jerusalem. The Western Wall is a very important place in the history of Judaism.

This girl is celebrating her bat mitzvah in a synagogue.

After the service, there is often a party for family and friends to celebrate this important day. After they have become bar or bat mitzvah, young people are considered to be young adults within the synagogue and the Jewish community. They are encouraged to take an adult role in the synagogue.

Sarah's story

Sarah, a Jewish girl, remembers her bat mitzvah, when she was thirteen years old:

All my family and friends came to our synagogue on the day of my Bat Mitzvah ceremony. I had been studying for several months beforehand. At first, I felt very nervous. But once I started reading from the Torah scroll, I forgot my nerves. . . .

Afterward, everyone congratulated me and we had a great party! Over the months that followed, I started to be treated like an adult in the synagogue, and I began to teach the younger children at Sunday school.

19

Hindu Upanayana Ceremony

There are sixteen different **ceremonies** that take place during a **Hindu's** life. They are called *samskars,* and they mark a change in a person's life. The tenth *samskar* is the *Upanayama,* or **sacred** thread, ceremony. It takes place when a Hindu boy is between eight and twelve years old. It is when he becomes a member of the Hindu religion. Only boys from certain castes, or social classes, can take part.

At the ceremony, the boy's head is shaved and he puts on a simple cotton wrap. Then, he is given a sacred thread and told, "Now you are a man." The boy then recites the Gyatri Mantra—a famous hymn from the Vedas, the oldest of the Hindu **holy** books. The sacred thread is a loop with three strands of strong cotton. The three strands **symbolize** three important forms of God (Brahman): Brahma, Vishnu, and Shiva. The boy wears the thread looped over his left shoulder and across his chest. He will wear the thread for the rest of his life. After the ceremony, there is a big party for friends and family.

This boy is wearing the sacred thread at his Upanayana *ceremony.*

Hinduism is the main religion in India. Hindus believe in Brahman, the supreme God. Hindus believe that the supreme God cannot be described or imagined in any way. So, to help them understand Brahman they worship the supreme God through gods and goddesses. They see Brahman in three roles—as a creator, a preserver, and a destroyer. Brahma is the creator of life while Vishnu keeps life going. Shiva is the part of the supreme God responsible for the death of living things.

This statue is of the Hindu god Brahman.

Hindus also believe that there has to be both male and female parts to the supreme god. Therefore, goddesses are also important in Hinduism. The female is often the opposite of the male. If the god is harsh, then the goddess will be kind. There is a Mother Goddess who can be worshiped in different forms. She can be seen as Durga or Kali, and is also Shiva's wife, Parvati.

Quinceañera

In many Latin American countries, such as Cuba and Mexico, girls celebrate their *quinceañera* (KEEN-say-ah-NYAIR-ah) on their fifteenth birthday. Sometimes it is called the *quince* or *quince años*. It is seen as the start of womanhood. Traditionally, after her *quinceañera*, a girl was thought to be ready to marry—although today, most girls prefer to wait until they have finished their education before getting married.

The *quinceañera* is often celebrated in the United States, too, especially among families who originally came from Latin American countries.

Family and friends gather for a quinceañera celebration in Mexico.

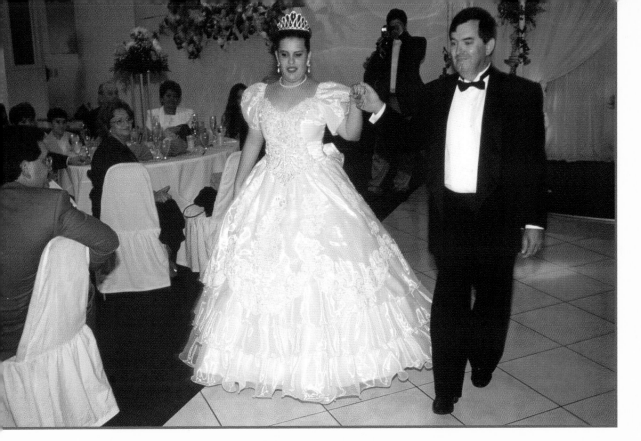

A father takes his daughter to her quinceañera *party.*

Traditionally, the *quinceañera* is a very elaborate and splendid party, much like a wedding. Families may save money for many years to give their daughters a memorable party. The girl chooses a gown in white or pastel shades. A hairdresser comes to do her hair. On the day itself, there may be a short service in church, but the celebration is mainly a nonreligious, family gathering. The girl's mother crowns her with a jeweled tiara. Her father takes away her satin slippers, a **symbol** of childhood, and gives her instead a pair of woman's high-heeled shoes.

Some girls are offered the choice between a *quinceañera* celebration and a car. By choosing the *quinceañera,* a Latin-American girl maintains her cultural traditions and celebrates her heritage.

Japanese Coming-of-Age Day

In Japan, *Seijin No Hi,* or Coming-of-Age Day, is a national holiday celebrated every January. It marks the coming of age of young men and women who have reached their twentieth birthday that year.

Young men wear a new suit for the special day. Young women dress in traditional, brightly-colored *kimonos* called *furisode* (foo-ree-soh-deh). Celebrations are organized by local governments, schools, or businesses. There may be speeches by important local people, congratulating the young people on becoming adults. They are given a special gift to remember the day, and they promise to become responsible members of society. After the **ceremony,** they may visit temples or shrines, or celebrate in town with their friends.

Young Japanese women wear beautiful kimonos *for their Coming-of-Age Day.*

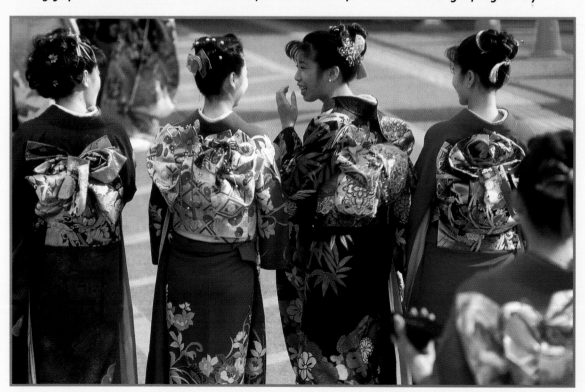

Seijin No Hi is a bright and spectacular sight on a winter's day each year. The ceremony dates back to the 8th century. Then, young boys from powerful families took on adult clothing and hairstyles. Coming-of-Age Day was made a national holiday by law in 1948. It helped to build up people's spirits as Japan was recovering after World War II.

Coming of age in Korea

Korea also has a Coming-of-Age Day, on the third Monday in May. Boys' long hair is tied into a top knot and they are given a *kat,* a traditional Korean hat made of horsehair. Girls have their hair put up and secured with an ornamental hairpin called a *pinyo.* There are great celebrations for family and friends.

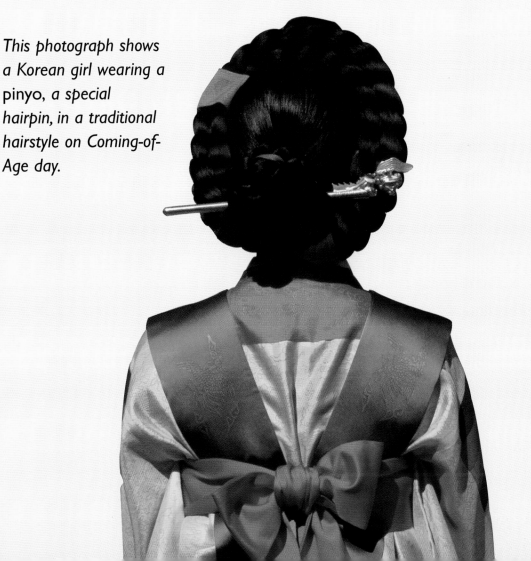

This photograph shows a Korean girl wearing a pinyo, *a special hairpin, in a traditional hairstyle on Coming-of-Age day.*

New Rituals from Old

In the past, many young people marked the change from childhood to adulthood within their religion. Others marked it by starting work. Young men often learned a trade, or job, as an apprentice—a kind of trainee. An older man would teach the apprentice boy the skills he would need, guiding him into the new world of work.

These traditions are no longer common in many parts of the world. Many people follow no religion, and young people may continue in education long after their bodies are grown. Some families are starting to recognize the need for new **rituals** to mark the change from childhood to adulthood.

A young apprentice learns engineering at a school in Manchester, England.

Some people are making new rituals, often taking ideas from **aboriginal** and African **initiation** rites. Fathers may take their sons into the forest for a camping trip when they reach **puberty.** The men's movement in the United States has developed new rituals for men and boys, such as drumming and chanting together and learning survival skills in the wild. These rituals help boys learn about becoming men. They also help boys develop bonds with older men, so they feel a part of a male family of **generations.**

This young Christian woman is reading a prayer.

New religious rituals

Some women are seeking rituals for girls' life events that conventional religion has ignored—for instance, the start of their **menses. Jewish** and **Christian** woman have written new prayers and adapted traditional ones to mark this time. They are celebrating the moment when a girl's body becomes a woman's, enabling her to become a mother in the future.

Growing Up, Moving On

In many countries in the West, including Great Britain, Australia, and the United States, many people no longer belong to religious organizations. So, many young people mark their coming of age, or growing up, in a nonreligious way, with a special birthday party when they are either 18 or 21. This birthday marks the beginning of adulthood.

For many young people, leaving home is an important move toward adulthood. Some leave home to go to college. Others leave home when they are working and can afford to pay their own rent. Many young people start by sharing an apartment with a few friends. Then, they have to do their own shopping, laundry, and housework, cook their own meals, and decide for themselves when to go to bed, get up, study, and go out.

A French teenager votes in her first election. Voting is an important right for young adults.

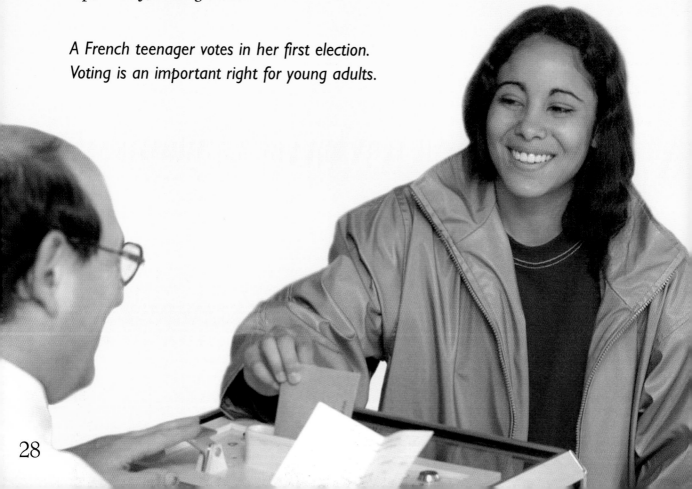

The start of adulthood is an exciting time. Some young adults feel a mixture of happiness and sadness at leaving behind their childhood. Becoming an adult brings new responsibilities—but it can also bring new beginnings and new freedoms.

Rights by law

In each country, the law gives new rights to people when they reach adulthood. They are allowed to do things that children cannot do. For example, they can vote, learn to drive, or get married without their parents' consent. Once a person has reached the age of adulthood, they can make their own decisions. The age when the law allows each of these things varies from country to country, but usually it is some time between fifteen and eighteen.

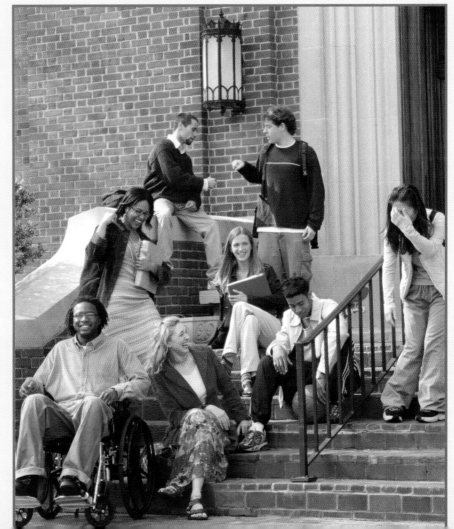

Students meet their friends outside of their college.

Glossary

aboriginal relating to the native peoples of Australia. Aboriginal people are called *aborigines*.

ancestor relative in the past. Grandparents and great-grandparents are ancestors.

Anglican person who belongs to a branch of Christianity including the Church of England

baptism act of welcoming someone into Christianity

Buddhist person who follows the way of life taught by Buddha, who lived in ancient India about 2,500 years ago. Buddha was not a god, but a man. He taught his followers how to live simple, peaceful lives.

ceremony special ritual and celebration

christening act of welcoming a baby or child into Christianity and blessing his or her name

Christian person who follows the religion of Christianity, which is based on the teachings of Jesus Christ. Christians believe that Jesus was the Son of God.

circumcise cut away the foreskin, the skin that covers the tip of the penis

clan group of people with common ancestors

generation all the people born around the same time

Hindu person who follows Hinduism. Hindus worship one god, called Brahman, in many forms. Hinduism is the main religion in India.

holy special, because it has to do with God or a religious purpose

initiation bringing someone into a new group or community

Jew person who follows the religion of Judaism. Jews pray to one god. Their holy book is the Hebrew Bible, sometimes called the Old Testament by Christians.

menses monthly bleeding that starts when a girl reaches puberty

Methodist person who belongs to a branch of Christianity that began in the 18th century

monastery all-male religious community

monk member of a monastery, an all-male religious community. Monks devote their lives to God.

Muslim person who follows the religion of Islam. Muslims pray to one god, whom they call Allah.

myth traditional story, often about supernatural beings, and sometimes used to explain why natural events happen

nunnery all-female religious community

orthodox group that strictly follows a religion

puberty when a girl's or boy's body changes into an adult's

ritual set of actions always done in the same way. often as a religious ceremony

Roman Catholic Christian who follows the leadership of the pope in Rome

sacred another word for holy

symbol picture, object, or action that stands for something else

synagogue Jewish place of worship

More Books to Read

Behar, Susan. *Growing Up.* Chicago: Raintree, 2001.

Miller, Jay. *American Indian Festivals.* Danbury, Conn.: Children's Press, 1996.

Pirotta, Saviour. *Jewish Festivals.* Chicago: Raintree, 2001.

Sita, Lisa. *Coming of Age.* Farmington Hills, Mich.: Blackbirch Press, 1998.

Index